FREEDOM LIFESTYLE

Building an Empire through Network Marketing

DEBORAH LOBART

BALBOA.PRESS
A DIVISION OF HAY HOUSE

Copyright © 2020 Deborah Lobart.

All rights reserved. No part of this book may be used or reproduced by any means, graphic, electronic, or mechanical, including photocopying, recording, taping or by any information storage retrieval system without the written permission of the author except in the case of brief quotations embodied in critical articles and reviews.

Balboa Press books may be ordered through booksellers or by contacting:

Balboa Press
A Division of Hay House
1663 Liberty Drive
Bloomington, IN 47403
www.balboapress.com
1 (877) 407-4847

Because of the dynamic nature of the Internet, any web addresses or links contained in this book may have changed since publication and may no longer be valid. The views expressed in this work are solely those of the author and do not necessarily reflect the views of the publisher, and the publisher hereby disclaims any responsibility for them.

The author of this book does not dispense medical advice or prescribe the use of any technique as a form of treatment for physical, emotional, or medical problems without the advice of a physician, either directly or indirectly. The intent of the author is only to offer information of a general nature to help you in your quest for emotional and spiritual well-being. In the event you use any of the information in this book for yourself, which is your constitutional right, the author and the publisher assume no responsibility for your actions.

Any people depicted in stock imagery provided by Getty Images are models, and such images are being used for illustrative purposes only. Certain stock imagery © Getty Images.

Print information available on the last page.

ISBN: 978-1-9822-4866-6 (sc)
ISBN: 978-1-9822-4865-9 (hc)
ISBN: 978-1-9822-4864-2 (e)

Library of Congress Control Number: 2020910007

Balboa Press rev. date: 06/09/2020

Gabriella and Bobby, dream big. I believe in you.

The biggest adventure you can take is to
live the life of your dreams.
—Oprah Winfrey

CONTENTS

Introduction xi

Chapter 1	Your Why	1
Chapter 2	Vision Board	5
Chapter 3	Goal Setting	11
Chapter 4	Cold Market	19
Chapter 5	Social Media	25
Chapter 6	Hot Prospects	37
Chapter 7	Initial Meeting	45
Chapter 8	Handling Objections	53
Chapter 9	Belief	61
Chapter 10	Duplication	67
Chapter 11	Leadership	71
Chapter 12	Work-Life Balance	81

Appendix 89
Acknowledgements 111
About the Author 113

INTRODUCTION

From a young age, I always dreamed of having this "big" life. I was tired of working for others and having someone else dictate my schedule. However, owning a business also required a lot of money and time—two things I didn't have. So I'd often wonder what the solution was for me. Do I work a job? Start a business? What would be the best way to create an income that gave me *freedom* so that I didn't need to sacrifice time with my family?

Then a door opened for me: network marketing!

I'd always heard about it, but I'd never looked into it in depth. I just knew that there was no ceiling on how much I could earn, and that really appealed to me. But there were many misconceptions about this business model. I couldn't understand why, though. At first glance, all I could see was the brilliance. An opportunity to work from home, on my own schedule, and earn a passive income? What's not to love about that? The only stipulation was that I had to work hard and take consistent daily action, which was fine with me. I had no issues working hard. So without thinking twice, I trusted my intuition, jumped in, and never looked back!

I started dreaming about the possibilities.

- What if I never have to wake up to an alarm clock again and take long dreadful commutes but rather wake up *any time* of the day, feeling excited to design my schedule the way I wanted to instead of going to a job I hate?

- What if I can work until noon and then spend the rest of my day at my favourite park with my daughter and not have to ask a boss for permission?
- What if I can own my dream home and book a spontaneous vacation to Italy without living paycheck to paycheck anymore?

These thoughts excited me to no end.

I literally picked up every book on network marketing I could get my hands on and started listening to CDs in my car at every opportunity. Momentum was picking up in my business as my schedule started getting busier and busier. The more people I shared the opportunity with, the bigger my business grew.

However, my first year in network marketing was a horrifying experience. I made only $3,000 the *entire* year! But I would pick myself back up by saying, "It's a business, Deb. There's no such thing as an overnight success. It takes time. Be patient." But even with this positive talk, I started hearing negative reactions from people around me. My husband not only started to question why I was still continuing, but when I took my paperwork to my accountant's office, he laughed at me. He told me he'd never seen anyone make money in this industry. Although this was hurtful, I didn't care. I used it as fuel to *keep going*. I was relentless. No one was going to steal my dream or tell me that what I was after was not possible.

Within two years, I ascended to top ranks and was now exceeding the full-time income I had ever made previously at any past J.O.B (a.k.a., "just over broke"). I was darn proud of myself—because now I had a "freedom-based lifestyle," which I had desperately craved. And I'm proud to say that with hard work, persistence, and daily action, *you* can do it too!

I will admit, though, when I joined this industry a decade ago, I found it challenging to obtain the business training I needed to thrive. So, I created this book with you in mind to help you get to the *bottom line* on what I believe are the "essential ingredients" you need.

Are you ready? Let's get started!

Deborah, XO

Activity without purpose is the drain of your life.
—Tony Robbins

CHAPTER 1

YOUR WHY

Our *why* is the *reason* we say yes to this opportunity. Should we want to make this business into a full-time passive income—I often tell people that our why needs to be connected to our heart—because times will get tough. And in order to keep going, our *why* needs to be strong. It should make you cry.

When I started my business over a decade ago, I had a strong reason why I was doing this business. It was very powerful. While I was on maternity leave with my first child and my daughter was about nine months old, I had three months left to go back to a job where I worked in sales and the hours were evenings and weekends. Not really an ideal schedule when you're a new mother. So, any time things got challenging in my business—say, somebody decided to quit or my paychecks weren't as big as I wanted them to be—it would have been easy to get discouraged, right? I did not, however, because my *why* was connected to my heart. Anytime I thought, *If this business does not work for me, what's my life gonna look like?* I just thought that I'd have to go back to my full-time job and I was not going to be able to put my daughter to bed. And that would be very tough for me. Therefore, *not* being successful was just not an option.

Here's what I want you guys to do: once you're done this chapter, take a sheet of paper and spend ten to fifteen minutes brainstorming why you are doing this business. I want you guys to get crystal clear on this, because the clearer you are and the more reasons you have, the more motivated you're going to be to keep going when times get tough. And just so you know, success in any industry is going to be a challenge. For example, did you know that millions of books are published each year, and yet only 0.02 percent of them make over $100,000 per year in sales? Did you know that fewer than 2 percent of actors can make a full-time income for more than five years? Did you know that fewer than 7 percent of real estate agents make over $100,000 a year?

Yet, nobody would ever discourage somebody from becoming a real estate agent. The reason I'm telling you this is that success in any industry is going to be difficult, but your *why* is going to drive you. Here's an example of a weak *why*. Let's say someone answers, "Money. Money is the reason I want to do this business." But what is it about money? Do you want extra money to do some extracurricular activities with your kids? Is it going to allow you to pay bills so you're not struggling each month and you're not short? Is it going to help your parents? Maybe they need help every month, and you're going to be able to give that support to them.

Your *why* needs to be clear, and it needs to be connected to your heart. Often, when I see people struggle, it's because they have a weak *why*. Here's another example. Let's say your company offers you the incentive of a car bonus. You're now able to buy a car, but you already have a car, and it is running fine. It gets you from point A to point B. So, will having another car get you out of your comfort zone? Much of what we do makes us stretch outside our comfort zone. You want to get comfortable getting uncomfortable, but the only way to do that is to have that strong *why*.

I want you to put down this book and spend a few minutes brainstorming all the reasons why you're doing this. Spend a few minutes creating your *why* (at least twenty reasons), and I will see you on the next page.

The secret to having it all is believing you *already* do.
—Unknown

CHAPTER 2

VISION BOARD

Creating a vision board is a great way to help you bring your goals into reality. It gives you something to look at every day and, which will help program your goals into your subconscious mind. This allows you to subconsciously start taking daily actions to bring you closer to achieving what you want.

You're going to want to get a few basic things: scissors, tape, bristol board, and images (from magazines or online).

Cut out all the images that you want. Keep in mind, they can be tangible, like a bigger home with more land and a swimming pool, or maybe you want a boat or a specific car. However, some of your items might be intangible. Maybe you want freedom, or maybe you want to let go of your full-time job so you can spend more time with your family. Cut out the images of what you want your life to look like and just put them to the side.

Did you know that your unconscious mind holds anywhere from 95 to 98 percent of your mental capacity? That means if you have any negative beliefs, they are stored in your conscious mind, which is only 2 to 5 percent of your mental capacity. This is exciting because you can talk to yourself daily about how your business is growing, how you're loving the momentum, and how you're attracting all these amazing superstars to your team.

When we talk like this daily, it becomes our internal dialogue, and it gets stored in our unconscious mind, which is way more powerful than our conscious mind. Amazing, huh?

The best time to think about the information you want stored in your unconscious mind is first thing in the morning and just before bedtime. So, look at your vision board for the first five minutes of your morning and the last five minutes before you go to bed.

People are driven to do things based on how they will make them feel. So, when you're looking at your vision board, think about how you will feel when you walk across the stage and receive that award. Maybe one of your goals on your vision board is to train in front of a huge audience. Picture yourself doing what you want to do and feel the emotions you might feel when you do it. Will you have tears of joy? What will you be wearing? Make things as real as possible. When you get your senses and emotions involved and combine them with income-producing activities, your dreams will become your reality.

Get some sticky notes, jot down your goals, and post them all over your house. That's what I used to do. It was funny, because when I'd have friends and family over, they'd say, "Wow, you have some big goals!" I plastered my goals everywhere. I'd have sticky notes on my fridge, all over my desktop, in my car, and in my wallet. This ensured they were *highly* visible. I would see them every day, which would remind me to look at my calendar and make sure I had enough meetings scheduled.

Divide your vision board in half. Put all your goals on one half, and on the other half, detail *how* you're going to make them happen. You might put pictures of yourself on the phone or maybe presenting the business in front of a large audience. You want to put the actual income-producing activities onto your vision board as well. When you combine the *how* with your *why* and look at them daily, your mind will understand that you can't achieve one without the other.

Meditate. Yup, I said it. I'll admit it: this was a huge struggle for me because I wasn't really consistent. But once I got into the groove of things (it takes twenty-one days to form a habit), I started to see a *huge* difference in the way I was thinking and feeling. I was calmer with the overall process. I just felt really good every day. And that's the key to doing well in this business—feeling good. That's because when we're in a state of positivity and love, we start attracting those qualities to our business.

Once or twice a day, close your eyes and take a few deep breaths. Sit comfortably and get yourself into a relaxed state. Start off thinking about what you're grateful for. Then, think about all the things you want to accomplish that day, that week, that month, and that year. Many of these things should be on your vision board as well.

Then, consider if there is anything else you need to do to make these things a reality? When you sit with yourself and quiet your mind, things will start to pop into your consciousness, like little whispers from the universe, telling you what else you need to do to make your dreams a reality. Then, once you're done, you can take a few minutes to journal what you thought about.

Fun Tip:

This is a great exercise to do with your family, as it gets your whole family on board with your goals. The more support you have from your family, the easier things will be. In addition, they'll be holding you accountable.

DEBORAH LOBART

I did this exercise with my kids. They had so much fun cutting out images, they even created boards for themselves. This is also something you can do with a team. It's a great way to bond and build community. You can play the movie *The Secret* (they talk about vision boards), have a bowl of munchies and some wine, and at the end of the evening, you can go around and showcase what you created. Super fun!

Do what is easy and your life will be hard. Do what is hard and your life will become easy.
—Les Brown

CHAPTER 3

GOAL SETTING

We need to know what we want to set a clear path on how to get there. The strategy will be different depending on whether we want to build a hobby or build an empire. These paths look very different. Since you purchased this book, I'm assuming that you want to build an empire. In this chapter, I'll give you the five steps you need to do to get crystal clear on what you want.

Step 1: Set a deadline.

Deadline strive urgency. When I was with my network marketing company, I had a deadline of December (which was one month before my due date).

I had already been in my business for about a year when I found I was pregnant with my second child. Before I knew I was pregnant, I was just dabbling with my business. I wasn't really sure of an exact strategy, and I hadn't set any deadlines. But once I was expecting, I set a deadline.

It is easier to build this business quickly than it is to build slowly. That's because building quickly creates momentum. It creates excitement. And when you have a packed calendar, you get more appointments, which leads to more sales and more sponsorships.

And that leads to a bigger paycheck and then more excitement. In this way, you create a cycle.

When you build your business slowly, without deadlines, you create no momentum. There's not as much activity, and as a result, you close fewer sales and you sponsor fewer people. This feeds doubt, because now you're getting paid less. Again, this business is easier to build quickly, and the way to do that is by setting deadlines. Therefore, I want you to set a deadline and be crystal clear about it. If someone woke you up at three in the morning, you should know exactly what your deadline is and be able to scream it out.

Business Tip:

Should you not achieve that goal, it's *okay*! There should never be pressure when it comes to your goals. When there's overwhelming pressure and we don't achieve our goals, we feel disappointed in ourselves. I know this is true because it happened to me. Therefore, be okay with whatever the result is. If you hit your goal, awesome! If you don't, you can try again next month. No big deal. Life will go on. Detach yourself from the outcome.

Step 2: Set monthly, weekly, and daily goals.

Let's say you have a monthly target of $5,000 in revenue. You want to get really specific about what you're after. I always set a number. However, I would always set a bit of a *stretch* goal. So, if I wanted $5,000 in revenue, I'd set a goal for $6,000, and then I'd divide that number by four. As there are four weeks in a month, then I'd have my weekly goal ($1,200). Now I knew a bit more clearly what I was after. I then broke that number down even further. I would take the $6,000 (in this example) and divide it by the number of days in that month. Let's say there are thirty days. That would give me a daily goal of $200.

Every company is different. So you'll know better than I could how you can achieve your daily goal. That's what I want you to do. Get crystal clear, because clarity is power. When we set vague goals, we get vague results. Hopefully, that will help you a bit.

Step 3: Determine how many prospects you need each month.

How many prospects do you need each month to present your opportunity to? It's a good idea to set a target of at least one to three business meetings per day. That will give you at least thirty to ninety prospects per month. We're looking to build this business fast, because fast equals a greater paycheck, which equals more excitement. So now the biggest problem (or the biggest challenge, I should say) is running out of people to talk to.

Step 4: Create a relationship list.

Start with your warm market. Your friends, family, friends of friends, and referrals should go on this relationship list, because these are the people you're going to work with at the beginning to get that opportunity in front of you. Remember, don't prejudge. You never know what's going on behind closed doors and who is desperately looking for a solution.

When I was building my business, I often created little stories in my head about why this person would not need my opportunity. I'd think, *Nah, this person is already making six figures. Why would they even be interested?* or *This person has their PhD. They're not going to get involved in network marketing.* I would decide for people, thereby withholding opportunities that could potentially change their lives. Who was I to decide for them and keep opportunities from them?

Later, I switched my mindset to believe that I was *offering* something to somebody. I was not "bothering" anybody, but I was offering a *gift*. Imagine you had a cure for cancer. Would you not go out and tell the entire world? If it could save someone's life, you would, right? Look at the opportunities you present with the same frame of mind.

Some people may be struggling to keep up with payments. We don't know what expenses people have. They might be struggling regardless of how much money they're currently making. Network marketing could be the difference that they're looking for. Therefore, write *everybody* you can think of on your list, and think: Whose life can I change?

Step 5: Keep adding people to your list.

Randy Gage, a top earner in the industry of network marketing, once said, "Two new contacts per day brings freedom my way." That became my mantra. I borrowed that mantra, and I said it to myself every single day. I would not go home until I had those two names on my list. This creates huge momentum, because if we don't have enough prospects to talk to, we don't have a business, right? The biggest challenge I see is that people declare massive goals, but then they don't have the activity to achieve them. To avoid having an empty calendar because you have no prospects to call, keep adding two new names each day. Whether you're at the start of your journey, the middle, or five years in, always be meeting two new people per day, and make that a commitment to yourself. Your confidence will rise when you have so many people to call.

Remember:

This business is *simple*.

I can't stress how simple the industry of network marketing really is. I'm not saying it's "easy." It's work for sure! But it is simple. The best copycat wins. All we do in this business is contact a prospect, book the meeting, present the opportunity, ask for the sale. Repeat, repeat, and repeat.

Two new people a day brings freedom my way.
—Randy Gage

CHAPTER 4

COLD MARKET

Prospecting is probably the number-one skill that you want to learn in network marketing. Once you target your friends and your family, who else is there to talk to, right? You really want to get good at building your cold market so you never run out of people to talk to. I actually had to build my entire business on a cold market because none of my friends and family were interested. In fact, they all thought I had completely lost my mind. I really had to prove to everybody that this business works, and I was on a mission to make sure that it was going to happen.

I did that through the skill of cold market prospecting. I'm going to go over six different steps that will help you become a professional in prospecting. It's very simple, and anyone can master this skill. Of course, in the beginning, we might stumble on our words. We may sound a bit crazy, and that's okay. To become great, we need to be good first, right? To become excellent, we need to become great. We all have to start somewhere.

Let's say you are in front of a prospect at a bank. If you are speaking to the teller, you're only going to be in front of that person for two minutes. On the other hand, perhaps you are at a wedding, where you're in front of a prospect—say, the person sitting beside you—for a couple of hours. The outline I'm going to give you works in either one of those scenarios, whether you're with somebody quickly and don't have much time to talk or you're with somebody for quite some time. The key is, whichever scenario you're in, you want to prospect them at the very end, just before you're heading out.

Step 1: Be in a hurry.

Let's say you're at the bank and you're talking to the teller. You're just making small talk. *At the end* of the conversation, you might want to say something like, "Listen, I'm in a rush, but …" Then finish your phrase. For example, "My husband's waiting in the car, but I just wanted to talk to you really quickly about something." The key is to be in a hurry so they're not firing a bunch of questions at you and you feel forced to tell them *everything*.

Step 2: Compliment that person.

You want to be sincere, so pick something that you love about that person. Remember, you don't have to prospect everyone. You can be selective. In fact, I encourage you to be selective, because you want people who have good energy. Try to bring only positive people into your life, because you're going to be working with these people, and you want to have a good relationship with them. Also, this business can get challenging at times. If that person isn't naturally positive to begin with, they may present a challenge later on. So compliment that person. Say something like "You're really hardworking" or "I love your personality" or "I love your energy." Whatever stands out to you is what you want to say.

Step 3: Make the invitation.

There are a few things you can say. Remember, you don't want to sound like a robot. You want to sound like yourself. I'll give you a few different things; use whichever one sounds the most natural to you. Or you can make up your own similar phrases; the following is just a guideline. You might say something like, "This may sound a bit random, but ..." That's actually a good way to make the invitation. "This may sound a bit random, but do you keep your options open in terms of earning another stream of income?" You might say something like, "This may sound a bit random, but I'm looking for two to three key people, and I thought of you. Would you be open to working on the side, from home, on your own schedule? Is that something that interests you?" Something along those lines.

Step 4: Get a commitment.

Once you make the invitation, you might say something like, "Are daytime hours good for you?" or "Are evenings better for me to give you a call so I can give you a bit more information?" Or you might say something like, "Are weeknights good for you, or do you prefer weekends?" The key here is to give people two choices so that they don't have an option to say no to your opportunity.

Step 5: Get contact information.

Now you want to be a bit subtle, you might say something like, "Okay, if you could just jot down your name and number, I'll give you a call" as opposed to "Write down your name and number, and I'll give you a call." See the difference? The word *jot* has been proven to get more people to provide their contact information. You might want to use that verbiage.

Step 6: Be in a hurry again.

I'll explain this one in the example below as I put all six steps together so you can get an idea of how they might flow.

Example:

Let's say we're at the bank. You're speaking to the teller, and he has a fantastic personality. He's smiling, you love his energy. You're only with him for about two minutes. You may have not found out much information about him, because again, you only have two minutes, but you're just taking a chance with him, and you're asking for an opportunity to meet with him. There's a fifty-fifty chance here. Remember, if you don't ask, there's no chance. You might as well take that 50 percent chance and ask him to see if it's a fit.

The conversation might look like this: "It was so great talking to you. Thank you so much for helping me out. Listen, I love your personality. I have to go, so now's probably not the best time, but I was just wondering—this may sound a bit random—but do you keep your options open in terms of earning another stream of income? I see you're so hard-working here, and I just love your personality." Then, wait for a response. If he says, "Sure," then say something like, "Okay, fantastic. Would daytimes be good, or would evenings be better for me to give you a call? Maybe just jot down your name and number, and we can discuss this further when you're not at work here, but now I'm in a rush."

You see how I put everything together?

Try not to make it so robotic, but rather blend in each step. These are simply general rules you want to follow. I hope this was helpful. This is the strategy I have used for years, and I have built a massive business in this industry based on cold-market prospecting.

If you follow this pattern, I promise it's going to work for you. Don't get discouraged if it takes a few tries, even a month, to get in the swing of things. It's okay. Just keep going and keep doing. Keep practising and practising. I promise you that at some point, it will flow off your tongue, and in time, you'll actually love prospecting.

No one is going to knock on your door and force you to be successful. You have to go out there and *fight* for it.
—Eric Worre

CHAPTER 5

SOCIAL MEDIA

This is a hot topic. I get questions all the time about social media. What should I post? What should I not post? Facebook, in particular, is an awesome *tool*. That's all it is—a tool to get in touch with people that you might not have spoken to in years, or to build new relationships. The idea is that you still want to do things the "old-fashioned way" and *build that relationship*. Once you've built a relationship, you can use any social media platform to get in touch with people so you can have a face-to-face meeting (whether in person, at a coffee shop, or via technology).

I'd like to go over some mistakes that I often see. There's really no right or wrong, so just keep in mind, this is my personal take from being in the industry for the past decade and what I have found to be great and not so great. I'll end off with some tips that I think will be helpful for you.

Mistake no 1. People remain inactive on their profile for a long time, and then suddenly, they join a company, and they start spamming all about their company and their opportunity nonstop, day after day after day, writing one, two, three posts a day. This turns people off. Ultimately, they'll either unfollow you or unfriend you. You don't want that to happen.

Mistake no. 2. The consultant writes a private message to a friend or prospect. Then they proceed to vomit information about their opportunity all over them. They send every last detail about their opportunity through messenger. At this point, the prospect has no real need to get in touch with you or respond to you, because you have already told them everything. I see this time and time again. The person on the other end will just ignore your message. So remember, be brief. Be that person who's going to create a bit of curiosity so people will end up following you and want to get in touch with you, because that will happen eventually. If you do things correctly, you'll see that people will start to follow you and send *you* messages instead of you reaching out to them.

Mistake no. 3. People post their company name. Now, you don't want to hide anything. You just want to be strategic, and you want to be effective with the way you're using social media. I'd say 90 percent of people break this rule. They brand themselves as their company and talk about their company. I've said this before: if you do this, people are just going to go on Google, and they're going to learn everything they need to know about your company and the opportunity you're offering. Then, if you do end up reaching out to that person, they won't need to respond because they know everything. This is a huge mistake.

Mistake no. 4. People start selling right away. Don't sell. Don't use your status to sell. Avoid saying things like, "Contact me, and I'll give you 50 percent off" or "Private message me if you're interested in an opportunity where you can work parttime from home." Never include any sort of *call to action* on your status. This looks too eager and desperate. Imagine how that looks to the prospect. How would you feel if you saw somebody doing that, posting everything about their product or service? Would you respond? Chances are you'd probably ignore them. Most people are not going to respond—I promise you that. Besides, that's the easy way out. Trying to talk to everybody on Facebook at once is the lazy way. You want to reach out to people personally and private message people to present opportunities.

Tip no. 1. Brand yourself. Who do you want to be seen as? I know I wanted to be seen as a mom, so I would post pictures of my kids and me out and about. I also wanted to be seen as someone who was into health and fitness. I also love to travel, so I post pictures of myself traveling. I want to show people I'm living life to the fullest, that I'm having fun, and that I'm an industry expert.

Think about five interests that you have aside from network marketing (or network marketing can be one of them). Then, each day, rotate what you post in terms of one of those interests.

Let's say you're really into baking. One day, you might post a healthy recipe of something that you baked that day. The next day, you might post something of you and something that you bought. Maybe you love fashion. You can post something about that. The point is to post something different every day. This way, you'll start to attract people from different walks of life who are attracted to you because of the things you like. They may not know anything about network marketing at this point, but they're going to start to follow you because you have shared interests. And then, that one day you end up posting something about network marketing, they're going to think, *Hmm, I really like what this person's about. We have a lot in common. I wonder what this "network marketing" thing is all about.* This way, you're creating curiosity and creating followers, which is ultimately what you want.

Many people ask me, "What's acceptable? What can I post about network marketing specifically?" People are confused. They'll ask, "What's good? What's not good?" The key is to be subtle. Don't shove your opportunity down people's throats. Make suggestions in a subtle, classy way. For example, if your company offers incentive trips and you find yourself traveling a lot, that's a great thing to post about. Post pictures of yourself on vacation somewhere with some of your team members having champagne. Or maybe you're having a team meeting at your house and it's in the backyard by the pool. You might tag that picture with the caption: "Just another day at the office." This way, you're creating curiosity.

Perhaps you've been promoted to a certain management level, or maybe you promoted somebody on your team to a certain management level. You might post a picture of you guys together. Maybe you were traveling to your company convention in Las Vegas. You can post a picture of yourself on the flight or at the conference. Basically, you're showing little tidbits of your lifestyle. Remember, what we're doing is selling a lifestyle. That's what we do. Your company is just the vehicle. Your company may be offering products or services, but it's the *vehicle* that's offering financial freedom and the freedom of time. So showcase your life to demonstrate the perks of doing this sort of home-based business. These are acceptable posts.

Make sure your profile picture is a picture of you, not a picture of your dog, your kid, or your house. Often, I'll look at a profile and think, *Who is this person?* because their face is nowhere to be found. Get professional headshots done. Use the same picture on your Facebook profile as your Instagram and your LinkedIn to be consistent and build your brand.

Don't forget to fill in the bio section on your Facebook account or your Instagram. It doesn't all have to be about network marketing. Remember, you're a human being. You're allowed to have other interests. You can put network marketing in there, but talk about your real interests. As I was saying, talk about things you love. Maybe you love chocolate. Be spontaneous and fun in your profile.

When we post things about our lifestyle, we make ourselves vulnerable. Some people may not like to be so open and expose their personal life all over social media, but you've got to remember: we're trying to draw people into our lifestyle, so we have to be open. People love others who are open. Not everything has to be positive. You could be having a rough day with one of your kids. They could be driving you nuts. It's okay to post something about that, but always give it a positive twist. You don't want to complain. Sharing such information makes you relatable because people can see that things are not always so positive in your world and you're just being real. People like that.

Tip no. 2. When I meet a new person, after building some rapport, before we part ways, I'll say something like, "We should keep in touch," and I'll turn my phone over to them and say, "Here, find yourself on Facebook." The next thing you know, they're adding themselves onto my Facebook account. Now we're Facebook friends. Then I'll turn on notifications, because now Facebook will place them at the top of my feed. Anytime they make a post, I'll be able to see it right away, and I'll be able to like it or comment. People like people who like them. It's all part of *building that relationship*.

You don't necessarily need a business page. I prefer to keep just a personal profile until you reach, say, 5,000 followers. At this point, I'd create a business page. Or perhaps you wish to wait until you reach a full-time income before you do that. However, in the beginning, you don't really want to talk about your company or anything like that. You can just use your personal profile. That's what I've done.

Tip no. 3. Develop a script. Say you want to reach out to somebody that you've built a rapport with and you're ready to talk to that person. You might send them a message and say, "Hey, I notice that we have so much in common. I wanted to see if you'd be interested in having a quick chat so I could tell you a bit more about what I do."

You can hop on Facebook audio or video chat. This is super easy, as you can connect with anyone globally for free.

Obviously, you're going to do this research regarding common interests beforehand. Look at their profile. You'll be able to see if they have kids. See what they're up to and what they like. Maybe they wrote something on their status one day about how they're looking for work, or how they really hate their job, or how their maternity leave is almost up and they have to return to work and they're upset about that. Do you see how we can gather so much information from a simple social media profile? Of course, not everyone may be interested in the business, but you might find a customer. Many customers will become consultants if they have a strong belief in the product.

Let's say you have several real estate agents on your friendslist, or maybe some teachers. You can reach out to a person who is a real estate agent and say, "Hey, I work with a lot of realtors, and I noticed you're in real estate. I'd love to connect and tell you a bit more about what I do. This could be right up your alley." Of course, you want to put your own personality into it so it sounds like you. This is all just to give you an idea.

See who likes your posts. Turn on notifications for all the people who are following you. Then, you can start to like their posts in return and comment on their interests. This is a great way to build a relationship. Remember, you don't want to have an agenda. You just want to be a nice human being. If somebody has a birthday, say, "Happy birthday." If somebody just had a child say, "Wow, welcome to parenthood" or "Enjoy parenthood. Your daughter is beautiful." Just love everybody where they're at. Put thought into how you comment, and be genuine. Remember, not everybody's going to be ready to join our opportunity on our schedule. They have to be ready when it's right for them. However, they'll definitely think of you if and when they are ready.

So love everybody where they're at. My friend, actually my best friend, didn't look at my opportunity for five years. She just wasn't interested. And then five years down the road, she got laid off after three years of being with a company and then it was her time. She was like, you know what, maybe I do want to join your business. Maybe this could be a fit for me. And after five years I finally showed her the opportunity and she joined. So a no now is not a no forever.

Tip no. 4. These are actually a few little tips about social media in general (whether it's Facebook, Instagram, or other platforms). People love consistency, so you'll want to make sure that you're posting daily. You don't want to post a bunch of things one day and then disappear for three weeks. Facebook will reward your behaviour if you're being consistent. They'll make sure that your post is highly visible and highly seen when you are consistent.

Facebook and Instagram love pictures with a bit of text. You don't want to post too much text because people just won't read it. Also, Facebook loves when you upload videos from your phone, not links from YouTube. They don't like it when you post too many links that direct people off of their site, and their algorithms will ensure your post won't be seen that much. When people are commenting on your posts, you want to respond to each person individually. Facebook prefers this as opposed to writing one response for every twenty comments.

Facebook loves it when you engage with your audience, for example, asking them questions. People love to answer questions and offer their opinions. I remember one time I asked the following question: "If there was one other language aside from English that you could teach your child, what language would that be?" It received a ton of responses. Again, it doesn't have to be related to network marketing. It can be about everyday life, and when you post that question, you're going to get a lot of engagement. Facebook loves such content and gives it priority.

Tip no. 5. When you are talking to somebody through Facebook Messenger or some other social media platform and the person is interested, speak to them right away using the app. If they're not free, try to get their phone number so you can message them. However, because technology has expanded so much, many people prefer to communicate via WhatsApp or Voxer instead. Be sure to ask them their preferred method of communication, and let them know you'll keep in touch that way—with the goal of scheduling an appointment to chat face to face.

You don't want to hide behind social media. I often see people who are a bit afraid to meet up with someone, so they'll just engage on Facebook Messenger, answering the person's questions and telling them all about the business that way. That's a good way to lose people. If you're afraid of getting on a call with a person on the phone, get on a three-way call with your upline, and that will help close the deal for you. And remember, while telephone can be effective, ideally, you want to meet face to face. People can feel your positive energy better this way.

That pretty much wraps it up. In summary, I want to highlight some key items that should help you in terms of using social media:

- Remember, although you're doing things "online," this is still primarily a relationship business. Use Facebook, Instagram, or other social media as simply a *tool* to connect with people (perhaps by private messaging people so that you can book a time to talk on the phone, in person, or via technology).

- Have a fun profile. Show people that you're having fun, that you love life, that you're inspiring. Your goal is to uplift people. Be that light in a dark world.
- Have five to seven interests you're going to rotate daily. Remember, every single day, you're going to rotate. It could be baking one day, fitness the next, and fashion after that. Then it could be your business, then your family, and then you're going to rotate that cycle all over again.
- When you meet people out and about, add them to your social media account, especially Facebook. Turn notifications on so you can start liking their posts and building that relationship.
- Facebook loves consistency, and they will reward your behaviour when you're consistent. Make sure you're posting consistently at all times, at least one to three posts per day.

At first, they will ask you *why* you're doing it. Later, they'll ask *how* you did it.
—Unknown

CHAPTER 6

HOT PROSPECTS

I began to study the people who had built large organizations, and I found that professionals focused on "building relationships" as one of their *core skills*. They developed this skill to make sure they never ran out of people. They started with a written list, but then they focused on committing to never stop adding to that list. I suggest making friends everywhere you go and finding a creative way to stay in contact with them. Collect business cards, friend them on social media, and have fun with it. Imagine how many contacts you would have over time if you did this consistently.

Now, although I was building relationships and my list was growing extensively (which gave me a big boost in confidence), I was still left wondering, "Where can I find more people *like me*?" Not someone who "needs" it but someone who's *hungry* for it. Because there are a lot of people who need it but are unwilling to do the work. Hungry people are.

It took me a while to understand that my business was in direct proportion to how much I was growing. I needed to focus on becoming the person I needed to make 100K rather than making a $100K. This is because we will attract who we are! I discovered I was sponsoring people who were just like me (broke financially but with tons of fears and limiting beliefs), so I was attracting all of these mini-mes running around!

Here's what I found. Great candidates have a few things in common:

1. Passion

It's genuine, not something they have to acquire. It's already in them.

2. Perseverance

We're going to constantly be knocked down, but as leaders, we get back up and keep pushing forward (vs. making excuses and playing the victim).

3. Integrity

Not only talk the talk but walk the walk. They live publicly the way they do privately.

4. Desire

Their desire to win is greater than the circumstances they're in. There are some people who will cancel a meeting right away if *anything* comes up. Success-minded people have such a desire. They believe "where there's a will, there's a way!"

5. Excitement

They love life and are so excited about the possibilities. Despite every obstacle thrown at them, they stay excited! When you find these people, this business becomes *a lot* of fun! But when you don't, this business is tough and challenging!

So, How Do You Find These People?

- Before you can sponsor success-minded people, *you* have to become this person.
- The people that are winning are sponsoring superstars. *We* need to be the change and do the work so we can attract the same.
- Rate yourself out of ten. What's keeping you from a ten? If it's a specific skill, identify it, study it, get into action, and practise until you've mastered it.

Note:

I have had people on my team who had never listened to any trainings or read any books and would complain that things weren't working out (and I'd try to motivate these people—huge mistake)! Pay attention to who you are spending your time with.

Network On Purpose

It's hard to network if you're hiding from the world. So you'll want to get out there, have fun, and don't come home until you've met two new contacts.

Twenty-nine ideas for finding hot *prospects*:

- Bookstores (i.e., self-help section).
- Spiritual centres—church, synagogue, etc.
- Events—plays, concerts, symphonies (people who go to these appreciate the finer things in life).
- University—Gen Y's are typically concerned with what they're going to do once they're done.

- Self-development workshops (i.e., Landmark, Anthony Robbins events, Robert Kiyosaki, etc.).
- Join a networking club—BNI is a great one.
- Join a gym—you may be able to get a free week pass and try a few to see which is best. You can network with the members, personal trainers, fitness instructors, and nutritionists.
- Starbucks—hang out at the same one often. You'll start to see the same people and can start small talk.
- Social media—look back at school yearbooks and wedding albums to jog your memory about who you haven't spoken to in a while and reconnect on Facebook, Instagram, LinkedIn, etc.
- Children's activities and play groups—those on maternity leave (for the most part) don't usually want to return to work.
- Referrals—three magic words when inviting someone for a coffee or party: "bring a friend!"
- Flights—request a middle seat (therefore, one prospect on each side).
- Restaurants—waiter/waitress didn't go to school for this and are often open to making more money.
- People in finance—they understand money and are usually open-minded to other streams of income.
- Daycare/school (teachers)—they already have the skill to teach and train. Many have a capped income and either work long hours or bring work home (having time freedom would be a dream come true for them)!
- Sales professionals—realtors, insurance brokers, personal trainers (they are already used to generating their own leads to make a living).
- Hair/nail salon—not only the workers, but you can strike up conversations with the people getting services in there.
- Neighbours/neighbourhood parks—if you have kids or pets, it can be easy to strike up a conversation. Get friendly and

build those relationships if you haven't already. Invite them over for tea.
- Dental hygienists—most of them work long hours (this is especially difficult if they have children and want to be home with them).
- Corporate world—most are tired of the typical nine-to-five schedule.
- Small businesses—the majority of them (if they're not in MLM) are exhausted and overworked, and they will never have the luxury of time freedom.
- Trade shows—you don't necessarily need to be a vendor (although it's also an option), but you can network with all of the attendees.
- Financial institutions (i.e., bankers)—they understand money and are often open-minded to other income streams.
- Malls—you can speak to not only the employees but the shoppers themselves!
- Clinics (doctors, massage therapists, etc.)—many of them make great money but trade their time for a paycheck.
- Parties—Anything you're invited to, *go*! These are awesome opportunities to mingle and meet a whole new circle of people you would have otherwise never met. Such events include engagement parties, weddings, bridal showers, and birthdays. Be open. Get to know people and get creative on ways to stay in touch with them.
- Coaches/trainers—again, they already have the skill to "teach and train" (which is essential to growing a large organization) and is a major perk if they decide to join you.
- Post office—a lot of the employees are tired of the typical nine-to-five schedule and desire more flexibility.
- Start a blog – by posting valuable tips and tricks on things you're passionate about, you'll potentially have people reaching out to you.

When you wake up each morning, be thinking, "Whose life will I change today?" You are offering a *gift* that can profoundly change the rest of someone's life. This is a lottery ticket.

If you think about it, there is no shortage of people! Anywhere you go, not only are there people in every direction, but many of them are looking for time or financial freedom (or both)! The goal is to strike up as many conversations with these people!

Mindset Tip

Prep your mind beforehand! Because guess what? When you're feeling awesome, prospects will be drawn to your energy, and as a result, they'll be more attracted to your opportunity. So note carefully how you are feeling each day. Are you irritable and frustrated or happy and excited? If negative feelings are more dominant, focus your attention on something that makes you happy *first*. It could be something as simple as going out for a walk and listening to one of your favourite mentors on Audible. Or it could be having a cup of tea while reading a chapter of your favourite book. The key is to take this time for yourself, without any guilt. In the long run, you'll notice that taking these moments to do what fills you up is more beneficial to your productivity than trying to force yourself to do something when you're out of alignment.

> I've failed over and over again in my life … and that is why I succeed.
> —Michael Jordan

CHAPTER 7

INITIAL MEETING

In order to have a great follow-up (which would be the second meeting), you will have to have a great "first meeting." I decided to divide this topic into two chapters because it's really important to go over what happens at the first meeting to know exactly what happens at the follow-up.

You want to remember that you are conducting an interview. Not everybody's going to qualify. I know that when I started my business, I thought maybe I should just sponsor everybody who had a pulse. But you don't want to do that. You want to be selective. This is because when you're trying to build your team and you're trying to pick up momentum, you want to make sure that you're sponsoring the people that your company needs, as opposed to the people who need your company. There's actually a big difference there.

So you want to sponsor people who are really hungry and driven, the kind of people who get things done. So you do want to offer the opportunity to everybody. But I often say that if you want to grow fast, you can't really help to change other people's lives until you first change your own.

Let's say you're at a coffee shop and about to go over the opportunity. Your focus should always be on that person. Not on your own agenda, not on what your goal is. Not on "I need such and such volume," so I need to close this person. You really just want to be a genuine friend. You want to get to know that person, especially if they're a cold-market prospect. You want to spend a few minutes just building a bit of rapport. You might ask them how their day was, what did they do that day, were they at work, how are things going at work? Do they love it there, or do they not like it there? You want to be a really good listener because the more information you have on their needs and the emotions connected to those needs, the more you can genuinely help that person.

So you want to listen for little clues so that you can have a little mental note as to what they said at the first meeting. So that when you do that follow up, whether it be at the end of your presentation on that first day or maybe it might take an extra couple of meetings after that. So you'll remember what they told you because everybody will join for different reasons. Some people will join because they need extra money to pay their bills. And then there are some people who just want a sense of community and want to build friendships. So you really want to get to know what it is that they want.

And I'm actually going to give you a perfect example. I used to mentor this girl on my team, and I remember going to an appointment with her and the prospect with somebody who traveled a lot for a living. The girl I was mentoring actually joined for many reasons, but one of the main ones was all the incentives to travel. So, when she was meeting up with that cold-market prospect and I was there, she talked a lot about the travel perks. But had she been listening to what this person's needs were, she would've known not to talk too much about the travel, because this person didn't really care, even though it was important to her. This is why you really want to get to know people. See what they like and what they don't like, and just pay attention to that.

Network marketing is specifically built for people who are already busy. Most people start network marketing businesses in conjunction with a full-time job. So, most people are really busy when they start. So you want to let people know that even if you're busy, you can do this business. And one of the things that you can do at your first meeting is talk about how this is only going to take about thirty minutes to go over. Of course, if the subject has extra questions at the end, then I'd be more than happy to answer as many questions that they have. But you want to honour their time, and you want to show people that it doesn't have to be a forty-hour work week with this. It can be five to ten hours a week as long as it's consistent. Let people know that right at the start of your meeting.

So, now you've done a lot of listening to them and their needs, and you've discovered who they are as a person and what they like and may not like to do. Now it's your turn to talk. Most of the time, when you're conducting these meetings, you are doing more listening than talking because you're really getting to know that person. But during the presentation, you want to basically take that lead for the next thirty minutes. This is your turn to talk. You can even say at the beginning, "I'm going to go over the entire presentation. If there are some questions, I'd be happy to answer all of them at the end, but I'll probably answer a lot of them during this presentation." Then go ahead and do your presentation.

When you get to the very end, you want to say whatever it is. Maybe it's a final slide that you're going over, and then you want to be quiet. Most people break this rule. They actually don't stop talking at the very end of their presentation. They just keep going. However, you don't want to keep talking after you're done your part explaining, because you're interrupting their train of thought—all their thoughts that they were thinking during the entire presentation. At this point, you do not know whether they are interested or whether they have concerns or fears. So ideally, you would want them to say the first word, but if they don't, then obviously, you're not going to just sit there and stare at them.

So you might start with, "So, was there anything that stood out to you?" Whatever they say will tell you whether they're interested. If they say something positive, you can reply, "Oh, okay. Why did you think that?" Then, they will elaborate, and now you're going to know exactly what hits their hot button, the thing that's really getting them interested. If it's something negative, or if they're not interested at all, then the meeting is over. You'd never want to convince anybody to do your business because it doesn't benefit them. It doesn't benefit you. You sincerely want to help people. So we don't convince anyone in network marketing. And you can even say that. You could be very open and say, "Listen, I'm not here to convince you to do anything. I sincerely want to help you. And I just want to know at this point if you have any concerns or questions so that I can eliminate any of those concerns." Because really, anybody can start a network marketing business as long as it is something that you're interested in. So you really want to get that clear.

Always ask open-ended questions. You can also ask, "On a scale of one to ten, where do you see yourself in terms of interest? Ten being 'Wow, this is something I definitely want to do. Let's get started' and one not being interested at all. You want to see where their interests lay, and if they answer anything above a one, then there's some interest. So you can work with that person.

Let's say they say five. Then you can say, "Oh, okay, what's keeping you from being a ten?" This will allow you to see what is standing in their way. Usually, it's three things that are standing in somebody's way. The first is time. They don't think that they have enough time to do it. The second is money. Maybe the startup cost of your company is just too much for them. The third is plain fear. It could be a fear of "I don't know enough people," a fear of "What are people going to think of me if I start something like this?" or a fear of "I'm not a salesperson." Usually, they have all these concerns, but it always comes back to fear.

You want to handle all those objections and concerns before they go home. If you don't, they're going to go home with all these fears. And then, if you do a follow-up after that, they're going to have to think about it still. So, if you eliminate it right at the first meeting, chances are, at the second meeting, you can sign them up. You're reducing the exposures that you have to meet up with them again by trying to get all the information and all the questions answered right at the initial meeting.

If they say "time," ask, "Well, how much time do you think this will take?" Because a lot of people just guess. "This is like another full-time job, and I already have a full-time job. Plus, I have kids, and I have all these extra activities. How am I going to fit everything in?" Most people don't realize this really is a part-time job. It can be. It can easily turn into a full-time job, but it could be a part-time job. And so I just asked that question to them, and then, usually after whatever they tell me, I say, "Listen, if you can find five to ten hours consistently per week, as long as it's consistent, you can build a network marketing business, because that's all it really takes."

It doesn't matter how busy somebody is. Everybody can find five to ten hours per week to build this sort of business if it's a priority. When you make something a priority, suddenly, you find time. Most people watch TV for five to ten hours per week. You need to find out if this is something they want, and if time is a concern, you could just say, "You know what? If time is your only concern but you really are interested in this type of business, you can eliminate that concern. Because if you can find five hours—a minimum of five hours consistently—you can do this business." So sort that out.

If they answer "money," then you can say, "Well, what's your budget?" You can turn that around. Most people do have the money if it's a priority. Let's say somebody's car broke down. Even if somebody really doesn't have the money, they'll find the money to repair their car. When something's a priority, somehow, someway, they will find the money. But the key to getting somebody to do something is to discover their hot button, what intrigues them.

If they say "fear" or it comes down to fear—fear of being a salesperson, fear of what people are going to think, or whatever the case may be—you can just say, "Listen, I totally get it." You can empathize with them. And you can say, "So many people are exactly in your shoes." Maybe it was you in their shoes. So you can use yourself as an example. And you can say, "Listen, this is what I did" or "This is how I handled this situation." If you know somebody, whether they're on your team or even on a different team, you can say, "I know somebody who was exactly in your shoes, and this is what they did."

That sums it up. You can either attempt to get them started right then and there, because some people can be ready. If you eliminate all those concerns and they say, "Yeah, I have no more questions. Yeah, you pretty much answered all my questions," and they are interested, then you can say, "So, should we get you started?"

If they still want to think about it, then, of course, we don't pressure anybody. At that point, schedule a follow-up within two to three days. You don't want to leave too much time because people change their minds. They go home, they talk to a spouse, they talk to a friend, and they're convinced not to do it. Therefore, you don't want to leave too much time between your initial meeting and your follow-up.

The more time you spend in your *discomfort* zone the *bigger* your *comfort zone* is going to grow.
—Robin Sharma

CHAPTER 8

HANDLING OBJECTIONS

This is the second meeting where you're going to be in front of the prospect, and they're probably going to be firing a bunch of objections. Now, there is nothing scarier to a new consultant than a prospect firing off a bunch of objections. My goal is to help you look forward to the follow-up so you actually get excited.

I'm going to go over some tips. Then, I'm going to go over what you can actually do in each scenario when somebody throws an objection at you.

Tip no. 1: Don't be too quick to say, "You know what? Next. This person's not interested. They're throwing a bunch of objections at me."

Objections are a *good* sign. It means that they're interested. They just want to get a bit more clarification, to find out if this is "truly" a concern to them or not. So learn to love hearing objections, because they're actually a good sign.

Tip no. 2: Honour the objection, but don't always believe it.

When somebody throws out an objection right after you ask them, "So, can you see yourself doing something like this?" the first thing that usually comes to mind is whatever they throw at you. It doesn't necessarily mean that that's the final say, right? People are just programmed not to say yes right away. And I know that was me. For example, when I went to my follow-up, my sponsor actually said to me, "So, is this something that you can see yourself doing?" And I said, "Well, I don't know. I'm a new mom. I don't know if I have the time."

It was the first thing that came to my mind. Meanwhile, at the back of my mind, I was thinking, "Is this something that I can see myself doing? I need a bit more information. I'm a bit skeptical. I need validation that this is a legitimate business model." I had other concerns, but the first thing that came to mind was "I don't know if I have the time," just to kind of buy myself a bit more time to go home and research a bit more. Again, tip no. 2: honour the objection, but don't always believe what they're saying.

Tip no. 3: Isolate the objection.

So if somebody says, "I don't have the time," then you want to isolate that objection. Say, "Okay, do you mind if I ask you something? If time wasn't a concern for you—let's say you had all the time in the world right now to build this business—is this something you could see yourself doing, or is there something else that's making you hesitate?" Okay, so you want to find out what else is going on in their mind by getting clarification and isolating the objection.

They might say, "Well, you know what? It's time, but it's also money. I don't know if I have the funds to start something like this." Now you're digging a bit deeper. You will now say, "If time and money were no object, is this something you could see yourself doing?" You're just trying to get to the root, to the bottom of it. And you can flat out say, "Is this something that you can sincerely see yourself doing? Let's say you had no concerns—time, money, or fear. Is this something that you would want to do? I just want to genuinely see if this is something you're interested in, because my goal is not to convince you to do this business. My goal is to help you. So I just want to know if this is something that you are interested in."

Those are the rules of thumb. Now I'm just going to go over some general concepts to help you answer an objection. The first concept is you want to relate to the person by using the terms "feel," "felt," and "found." For example, "I know exactly how you *feel*, Sarah. That's exactly how I *felt* actually. But here's what I *found*." You're building trust, you're building that relationship, and you're just relating to the person so they can see you're coming to understand their point of view.

Concept number two is you want to ask more questions, because when you ask questions, you're getting clarification, and it shows that you're actually listening to the prospect. You can say, "You know what? I totally get it. I was exactly in your shoes. This is what I found." Go over that. But then you can go into a question. You can say, "So let me just get clear on something. If time weren't a concern for you, could you see yourself doing something like this?"

The third concept is you're going to tell a story. You can use yourself as an example, or you can use somebody on your team or somebody that you know on another team, and you can just say, "So-and-so was exactly in your shoes before. This is what happened to her." You want to blend all those three concepts together. Relate to the person, ask questions, and tell stories.

This is something that I heard from Eric Worre. I absolutely loved this, so I wanted to share it with you. There are many objections somebody can throw at you. There are actually fifty-nine of them. Instead of learning how to answer every single one of those objections—that's going to drive you crazy—isn't it amazing to know that you can actually narrow every single one of those objections down to two?

The first one would be a limiting belief about themselves, and the second one would be a limiting belief about network marketing. So, all fifty-nine of those objections can be narrowed down to one of those two. For example, somebody might say, "Those things never work." That would be a limiting belief about network marketing. Or they might say, "You know what? I don't know if I could see myself doing that. I'm not a salesperson." That's a limiting belief about themselves. "I don't know if I have enough time." That's a limiting belief about themselves. "People at the top only make money." That's the limiting belief about network marketing. "I don't know if I have a big enough network" or "No one is ever interested in network marketing." These are limiting beliefs about network marketing.

I love that, because it actually shows that you can narrow down every single one of those objections. Then, all you have to do is think, "Okay, what is this person telling me? Which category is it?" Then go back into the concepts. Relate to the person, ask questions, tell them a story. Let's put all that together. For example, let's say somebody says, "You know what? I don't know. I'm not much of a salesperson." Now you know the person holds a limiting belief about himself. This is kind of like a fear.

You can answer, "I know exactly how you *feel*, Sarah. I actually *felt* the same way. But what I have *found* is that the majority of people who do network marketing have never been in sales before. In fact, I'd say over 80 percent of people who actually do network marketing have never been in sales. And some of the top income earners in this company have never been in sales before. So let me ask you a question. Is this your only concern? Is this something you could see yourself doing if that weren't a concern for you? Because it shouldn't be a concern. Many people are in your shoes." So now I have related to her. I asked her questions, and I told her a story.

I hope that was helpful. There's no real one-liner that I can give to you to show you what a follow-up looks like or how to handle a follow-up, because it takes practice. Repetition is the mother of skill, so you just want to keep doing it over and over and over again, and you're going to start to believe in yourself that this does work.

To go to a follow-up with more confidence, you want to ensure that you have plenty of other activity in your calendar. Whereas if you just have one or two meetings scheduled for the entire month and you think, "Oh my God, this person better say yes," your confidence drops. But when you have tons of activity and your schedule is booked solid with appointments, it's a big confidence booster.

The more you invest in yourself, the bigger your business gets. And that's the key, because people can't argue with you at a follow-up. When you're really passionate and knowledgeable about something, they're not going to be able to say anything, or they're not going to be able to be so skeptical, because they see that you really believe what you're talking about and you have that knowledge, you have that belief, you have that passion, and that is ultimately what's going to raise your confidence. But it does take time, so don't be hard on yourself.

To earn more, you must *learn* more.
—Brian Tracy

CHAPTER 9

BELIEF

Doubt is the opposite of belief!

You *can't* have doubt and belief at the same time. So how do we deal with doubt? When a new consultant joins, they're all excited! They see their destiny, *but* there's also an inside game going on too (which doesn't match their outside). They join, and then, within their first three months, all their prior mental conditioning and past experiences override their excitement! The voice in their head starts to take over and says things like, "What do you know about the business? What if you're not good enough? Smart enough? What if you don't fit in? What if you disappoint people?" As you can see, mindset directs the course of your business.

When you doubt your power, you give power to your doubt. That being said, doubt will always be there, but you can learn to manage it.

Here are four things you can do right away to *fuel* your belief instead.

1. Personal Growth

When someone is involved in a consistent income-producing activity yet is still struggling, there is usually a lack of belief in one of these four key areas.

a) Products

This one is obvious, but if one is not using the products or doesn't like them for that matter, it's going to be very difficult to recommend them to others. Make sure you stand behind your product and share them from a place of authenticity.

b) Company

Make sure you align with your company's mission, system of conducting business, and compensation plan. Also, plug into everything your upline or company hosts for you—this includes team meetings, calls, and conventions. This will instantly fire you up and fill your cup. There's nothing more inspiring than seeing other people who have been in your shoes before share their stories of how they became successful! Schedule all these important dates in your calendar ahead of time so there are no excuses.

c) Industry

Too many people have lost their own dreams, and they will try to take yours away too! If your battery is dead, you can't be positive for your prospects. But when you *believe* in network marketing as an industry and business model, nobody will question your opportunity.

d) Yourself

As you move up the ladder and start building a team around you, believing in yourself becomes more and more important. Now people are looking at you as their leader. This is when any old negative beliefs about yourself growing up may try to trick you that you aren't good enough to be in this leadership role (we obviously know this is a limiting belief and not true), but this is where we are going to want to boost our confidence.

No matter where you are in your journey, set aside thirty minutes a day of personal growth. I'm sure you're busy, so if you want to kill two birds with one stone, you can do it in the car while you're driving, working out, or cleaning up around the house.

2. Create a Goal Mantra

Repeating a thought to your subconscious mind (when it's mixed with feeling and emotion) is how to change a negative feeling into a positive one. I was once advised by a mentor of mine to create a goal mantra. This exercise helped me skyrocket my business when I stayed consistent with it.

So, on your phone (or on an index card), write,

"I am so grateful for having optimal health, awesome confidence, and a constant flow of money, time, and freedom in my life. I attract the right people and opportunities that will enable me to promote to _____" (fill in the title you want to achieve, along with the date of when you're going to achieve it by)! To program this into your subconscious mind, read this out loud five times in a row, five times a day (especially upon waking and before bed). Set reminders in your phone. You will slowly begin to shift your mindset. Duplicate this with your new distributors too. I often see many people trying to change outside circumstances when 80 percent of success is an inside game.

3. Surround Yourself with Successful People

To see the enormity of what this opportunity can do for you and your family, you'll want to get in front of top earners. Find five to ten other people who are successful that you admire, and get to know them. Maybe they have a similar career or personality to yours, or they are a parent like yourself. Go to their meetings. Mingle. Ask questions. Maybe you can reach out over social media or email and grab a coffee with them. Being around people who have what you want will fuel your belief and keep you focused.

4. Change Your Self-Talk

The saddest thing I see is when people quit too soon because they don't feel worthy. They bring their past into the future and don't believe they are capable of doing great things. If you ever feel this way, I want you to repeat these affirmations to yourself every morning:

"I am worthy!"
"I am wonderful!"
"I deserve this!"
"I am earning $10,000 a month!"
"Large sums of money come to me easily!"
"I am attracting new distributors to me like a magnet!"

Acknowledging that you are worthy of this success reinforces your subconscious mind to keep working hard for you. Your past is not your potential. Find ways to love yourself, because you were born for greatness! If you have kids, be that role model for them so that they too can believe in themselves and follow their dreams!

The richest people in the world build *networks*.
Everyone else is trained to look for work.
—Robert Kiyosaki

CHAPTER 10

DUPLICATION

Once people become distributors, they need a team! And to have a team, we need to duplicate. Duplication begins the moment you start talking to someone (what you say, what you do, etc). People are looking at you thinking they need to duplicate.

Duplication means keeping it *simple*! We have a tendency to overwhelm new distributors with information too fast, too soon, which causes confusion. Most people have never recruited people or had a business before, so they shut down and don't return our calls. Doubt can easily creep in, so take baby steps with people and teach them bite-sized pieces.

When people see that things are simple, this creates confidence. Confidence creates action. Make things easy, and you are well on your way to becoming a duplicating machine. So you want to make sure you're doing the right things with these new consultants right from the get-go.

Here are four important things you'll want to do when you sponsor a new distributor:

1. Get the new consultant into momentum right away.

This way, they can experience success when people are buying products or joining their team and start to visualize their business moving forward. This becomes fun for them, and they will want to continue that momentum. If you see they are procrastinating, you can say, "The good thing is this is your own business, and you get to decide how you want to run your business, but can I be honest with you? As busy as I am getting, I can't promise you that I'll have time in my schedule next month to go on these meetings with you. I've set aside time to help you now. So, did you want to wait or have your meetings now?"

2. Sponsor someone underneath them ASAP!

Because there's a mental shift. Their mind starts to think, "I got Mary underneath me, but what if Mary becomes successful and I quit?" They don't want to lose out, so this motivates them to stick around (even if their mind is telling them to quit). It also shows people the possibilities. It teaches them that sponsoring is not difficult. People usually have a mental block when it comes to recruiting.

3. Try to earn them a triple-digit paycheck within their first two months!

There's nothing that will fuel someone's belief more than a nice paycheck in the mail! They will feel like their business is moving forward. It will boost their confidence that they can do this, and they will feel that it's worth their time and energy.

4. Lead from the front.

Show them what needs to be done by being in the activity yourself. People will duplicate what you do, not what you say. Sometimes people spend so much time on training that they don't focus on what's most important. When people get started, we only have a certain amount of time to affect them before their mind gives in to doubt. Be a professional encourager. This will motivate them to keep pushing through and start duplicating.

Your legacy is every life you have touched.
—Oprah Winfrey

CHAPTER 11

LEADERSHIP

What is a leader?

A leader is someone who gets people to *willingly* step outside their comfort zone. So, when we take action and prospect our cold market or pick up the phone to book up our schedule, this inspires our team, and they duplicate! This is true leadership in our industry!

Growing our paycheck really comes down to stepping out of our comfort zones consistently! Think about what's been holding you back? What are you avoiding that you know you need to do? These are your fears. Unfortunately, this is what holds most people back from taking their business to that next level! According to Robin Sharma, in order to get rid of fear, you need to jump in and do whatever scares you right away!

In order to build a six-figure business, we need a team. Not only do we need a team, but we need leadership. We get paid the most by getting people to leadership levels, which means helping people reach the highest level of success! However, as they do this, many people make one *big* mistake, so please take note here.

Not everyone wants to be a leader, and we need to love and accept everyone where they're at (or they will leave). You might see greatness and potential for certain people to grow, and you may want to treat these people like leaders. But in fact, the majority of people don't want to become one. It's not their goal. Your job is to lead by example and see who follows. Those who follow want to be leaders.

We need to love and accept everyone where they're at!

Leaders Aren't Born. They're Developed!

It doesn't take talent or good looks to learn leadership, so you *are* in control! In fact, don't try to be perfect. Your team doesn't want you to be perfect, because they aren't! Let your team see you fall down! It allows them to feel they're not "alone" when it happens to them.

If you consistently work hard on yourself, not only will you grow into the person you've always dreamed you could be, but this is something that no one can ever take away from you and will ultimately give you more fulfillment! Money is just a byproduct!

As your income grows, so will the impact you have on other people's lives and your own family. When you quit, you are saying no to your team, your future team, your family, and the legacy you leave and to your dream! Other people's blessings are tied to your obedience!

Figure out where you are and where you want to be. Remember, you will attract who you are. So, if you want to attract someone ambitious and courageous, you must grow to be that person too! The more you learn, the more you earn!

Leaders Take Action

The difference between good and great is doing a bit more (showing up more, being around great mentors, etc.).

Creating a successful freedom based lifestyle is well thought out. So, every day, you'll want to reflect and be deliberate about what you want your life to look like. Envision it! Most network marketers don't set these intentions. They just accept their current lifestyle as is and "try" this thing called network marketing. Living in this unintentional way, they will never create what they want, and so they will never feel what they could feel.

Life is not a dress rehearsal. We don't get another shot at it. Hope is not a strategy. Therefore, to be successful, you have to *do it*!

Here's an exercise I once heard described by John Maxwell:

Before you go to bed each night, lie in your bed and say out loud to yourself, "Do it now" fifty times. Do it for the next thirty days. Guess what your first thought will be when you wake up. "Do it now!" How's that for getting yourself into action? Make sure to do this exercise!

Set an intention each morning. What do you need to do? Who do you need to call? Get specific and write it down. Having an intention prevents procrastination! The greatest way to improve your life is to take action and do something *today*, every day! You'll feel amazing!

Today is the *only* day. Yesterday is over. Tomorrow is maybe. But today is guaranteed. Pick one thing you want to be intentional with (e.g., making phone calls). Just take one step at a time. Take four or five things you want to work on, take that step, and be deliberate and consistent.

What Are You Duplicating?

Mirror Test: before you go to bed, ask yourself this question:

What would my organization look like if they did what I did today? Imagine you had three-way opportunity calls with five people, training calls with a hundred people, recruited two people, etc., and you had a thousand people in your organization. Awesome, right?

When the Going Gets Tough

You didn't ask for those struggles, but our biggest lessons are in these struggles. You were blessed with it so that you could be a blessing to other people! You'll often hear me say that "leadership is not about us"; it's about leading people to their destiny that they are longing to go, even in the midst of pressure. But to help others, we need to go through personal and spiritual growth. Your purpose will drive you through all of the tougher times! Anytime you have thought of quitting, revisit your vision board, stare fear in the face, and persevere! There is nothing like seeing your reason *why* come true!

Leadership Skills to Master

Skill No. 1: Empowering Other People

We don't need to be powerful. Rather, be empowering! You'll empower other people when you let their light shine and they see their own greatness! All you need to do is ask open-ended questions and listen. Let people figure things out on their own.

Skill No. 2: Listen to Your Heart

This is about being in your heart so you're present (not your head). We want to be of service to other people, where there's no judgement, just trust. Being vulnerable. Sharing that you didn't always have it all together. We all have "stuff," but it's about being who you are and taking off the mask. Speak truth, and always do the right thing—even when no one's watching.

Skill No. 3: Offering Feedback with Compassion

When you see a blind spot in someone, it's best not to beat around the bush. Ask if the person is open to hearing feedback. You can say something like, "May I share something I noticed?" People will never say no because they know this feedback is given by service. The key is *not* to make them wrong!

Skill No. 4: Holding People Accountable

Not just having "a conversation" but having one with *action*! For example, where would you begin? Where would you start? What would be your first step? How committed are you to taking that action? What are you committed to this week? Get them to take responsibility for themselves. Commitment is tied to integrity! They must do what they said they were going to do!

Skill No. 5: Acknowledgement

How do you show up with people that make them feel special? For example, recognition doesn't always have to be when someone is doing amazing. It could just be for effort! Send them an email or make a post on your Facebook group page about them for everyone to see. Acknowledgement goes a long way!

A Popular Leader vs. Servant

A popular leader is someone who has created success. They have lots of followers and a big team. They have a big vision and can articulate it. They are charismatic, and everyone likes them. They tell you what you want to hear when you want to hear it!

A servant leader is the exact same as the popular leader, *but* the one thing that separates them is they tell you the *truth*—what you need to hear, not just what you want to hear. They are courageous and tell you even if it affects your feelings temporarily to affect your future temporarily. The truth will set you free, but it will piss you off at first. However, they aren't afraid to share it with you, because they have a much bigger vision for you.

A popular leader leads with their goal in mind, but a servant leader leads with the consultants' goal in mind.

A popular leader is concerned about her image, what will people think. A servant leader is concerned about the consultants' image. She wonders, "How will this affect you?"

A popular leader focuses on being liked (because she thinks, "If you like me, you'll stick around"). A servant leader focuses on being trusted (because she thinks, "If you trust me, other people will trust me as well").

A popular leader delivers hype and motivation. A servant leader delivers content, because she wants you to be changed (because motivation dies down).

A popular leader always leaves a smile on your face. A servant leader always leaves their message on your heart. So, they're not just motivated, but she gets them to feel with their heart so they are feeling inspired to go out there and change the world.

Key Points to Becoming a Servant Leader

- Focus on the individual's goal, not your own: Get them to write it with dates and in the present tense. If you help them with theirs, you will automatically achieve yours!
- Speak to people as if they're rising leaders, not lucky followers. Speak to them as if they are a rock star (whether they are new or have been with you forever)!! Treat them as if you are lucky to have them on your team!
- Work on becoming better ourselves so we can pull the best out of someone else. It's really hard to pull the best out of someone else when you're not working on pulling the best out of you! That's because when you can spot the best in you, you can do the same for others.
- To not be intimidated by someone growing; keep helping people get to their next level of growth. Be excited about what you can help pull out of them.
- Believe in yourself so you can believe in others (more than they believe in themselves), and create massive significance!
- People don't follow titles; they follow courage. Servant leaders have a mission and a higher calling. They are passionate about what they do. They feel things others don't feel. They are *too* passionate that others can *not* question if they're "sure" about what they're talking about. They get their energy from their passion, and their passion is to make an impact!

You can't pour from an empty cup. Take care of yourself *first*.
—Unknown

CHAPTER 12

WORK-LIFE BALANCE

What I learned is that *instead* of chasing my goals *first*, I decided to focus on my own health and happiness *before* tackling my goals. This gave me energy and let me work from a state of peak performance so I could accomplish more. By doing it the other way, I felt tired, stressed, and unhappy—and as a result, I got very little done.

I've compiled a list of ways for a consultant to manage themselves and their days to have a better work-life balance.

1. Have a Morning Routine

   a. Wake up early

   "Early" means with the sun or before. This gives a jumpstart to your day. The first five minutes will be tough if this is new to you, but after you've made this a habit, you will feel like you have more time in your day. This has been one of my favourite morning rituals by far!

   b. Exercise

   Fresh oxygen to your body will increase your energy for the day, which is why top network marketers who exercise are more productive. You can also listen to your favorite audiobook during this time and kill two birds with one stone (download the Audible app).

c. *Prime*

Take ten minutes to close your eyes, quiet your mind, and focus on your breathing. When you feel calm, place your hand on your heart and think of three things you are grateful for. They don't have to be big things; they could be little things, like a hug from your child. End with three goals you want to accomplish—it could be for this week, this month, or this year.

d. *Get proper nutrition*

I like to have my hot lemon water before I eat, as it bathes my body in alkalinity—you may want to try this. Otherwise, drinking enough water throughout the day is key. It's really the simple things that make a huge difference. Drink half your body weight in ounces. And of course, go fresh! Having lots of fruits and veggies gives us energy. The more colorful, the better. Berries and leafy greens are packed with antioxidants.

e. *Take cold showers*

This is not exactly a gentle way to wake up, but cold water promotes a sense of health and wellbeing. It will instantly boost your mood.

Bonus Tip

Don't check emails or social media first thing upon waking, as this increases stress and cortisol. Instead, schedule this in.

2. Self-Care

How do you take care of yourself? Or is your focus on taking care of your spouse, kids, and team?

On airplanes, they always talk about putting the oxygen mask on yourself *before* you help put it on others. Self-care is similar in that it needs to be a top priority, before care for anyone else. We can't pour into others if we are not feeling our best first!

Ideas

- get a massage
- eat well
- take a nap
- have a Jacuzzi
- meditate
- do yoga
- jump on a trampoline
- dance
- hang out with good friends
- read a book
- write
- go for a walk
- listen to high-level mentors like Abraham Hicks
- have fun, whatever "fun" means for you!

How Often Should You Replenish and Rejuvenate?

As often as your body requires it! Listen to your body! Recognize symptoms. If you're feeling tired, rest. If you have a headache, it could be stress. If you're not feeling excited, do something that is *fun* before getting to work. This does wonders for your energy and mood. I use to think taking time for me was a waste of time, until I started to get sick more frequently. Once I started incorporating self-care into my daily routine, I was amazed at how much better I was feeling *and* how much more productive I was. For a long time, my "to-do" list was my top priority, and I never felt good. I always felt like I was living in the future, robbing me of precious moments and constantly feeling burnt out and unhappy. I wasn't aware of what my body was trying to tell me. Now I know better.

Self-care is self-love and is never selfish! Please take time for *you*!

3. Set Boundaries

Usually, the ones who say yes to everything have a chaotic house. Write one thing down that you can (or want) to decommit from. And be honest, because it's not in your best interest for your life and business to be juggling a million things. This is key for your mindset and health.

4. Manage Your Emotions

Make your feelings a *top* priority and a goal each day! Because when you feel good, you will positively affect *more* people! So take note. What are you currently feeling? Are you feeling excited, or do you feel frustrated? Happiness is a daily choice that we can control! Anytime you don't feel your best, be a detective. Whatever you *think* you are, you're not! It's just a story you created yourself, that's giving you limitations and lowering your energy. If you want to change this, try putting yourself in a peak state and focusing on what you're grateful for instead. Gratitude is the polar opposite of fear and will instantly raise your vibration. And please remember: happiness is not in that final destination of achieving that big goal. *It lies in the journey*! Having fun while we build this business attracts people to our opportunity so much more easily than trying to control the outcome!

5. Keep a Journal

Write about what's been successful, anything you were inspired by or even learned. You can always reflect and look back. Seeing little wins is so motivating! Plus, if you have a lot on your mind (perhaps before bed), having a brain dump is very beneficial for *restful* sleep!

Life has no *limitations* except the ones you make.
—Les Brown

APPENDIX

PROSPECT TIPS

Common Objections

"Is this MLM?"

Yes, it is! Sounds like you've had some experience with it. Tell me more about it! (The idea is *always* to answer their question and then answer their question with another question to get them talking). You can then say, "Most people have 'heard' of the idea but have never sat down with someone to get properly informed."

Is this one of those "pyramid things"?

"Pyramids? What do you mean by that exactly?" (Let them explain. Most won't have a proper answer.) You can then say, "Pyramids are illegal, since there is no distribution of a product. You only get compensated on people. I on the other hand, get paid based on volume of sales.

I don't know a lot of people though!

"It's always great when you know a lot of people, but even if you did, you would eventually run out of those people too! So, the idea is to master the skill of networking. That way you always have people to contact! And this is a skill that anyone can learn. There are many people who have moved to a new town who have gone on to build massive organizations without knowing a single person."

"I am just way too busy!"

"I totally hear you! I was in your shoes before working a full-time job with a family at home (show empathy in a situation that relates to your circumstance). But I've learned that you can build this with as little as five to ten hours per week, as long as it's consistent. Looking at your schedule, can you find five to ten hours per week?" You want to show them that by temporarily giving up some time now, they can escape the rat race and have more time later on.

But there are way too many consultants. I hear about that company everywhere!

While that may be true, people are not necessarily joining "the company"; they are joining *you* (the messenger). If you believe in the business model and your product, people are going to join you based on your belief and passion!

Have you made any money yet?

Every month is different, just like *any* other business would be! And the great thing about it is the more I put in, the more I get out of it." (Remember, you don't need to give them exact figures, just like you wouldn't if you had another type of business. This is a very personal question, so you have the right to be vague). If you are brand new, you can always say, "I just started the business, and any business takes time to generate income. However, I can introduce you to my upline, who have made money already and are very successful."

How long does it take to reach a full-time income?

"It really depends on how much time you commit. Obviously, the more you put in, the more you get out. While there is no guarantee—because everyone's journey is different—there are people who reach a full-time income in as little as a few months, and there are some who take a few years. It really depends on you and how big your 'why' and drive is."

But you started early. That's why you're successful!

"I can give you several examples of people who joined recently and reached success, and then there are people who joined years ago who are still in the same spot. We don't measure how successful one is based on how long they've been doing it but rather how many people they've spoken to about the opportunity."

Very few make it in that industry!

"Isn't this true in any industry, though? Have you checked out the success rate of realtors who make over $100K? Less then 7 percent. Also, more than a million books are published each year—only a thousand of them make over 100k a year. That's a 0.02 percent success rate. The only people who fail are those who give up!"

"But I am not a salesperson!"

"Awesome, the majority aren't either—you are not alone! We have people from all walks of life. The only criteria is that you love helping others, you're hard working and coachable. The rest you will learn as you earn!"

CONSULTANT TIPS

Common Questions

Do you need a proper workspace?

You should have a designated (neat and tidy) place to do your work. If you have to move dishes, this is not a place to do work. A cluttered desk equals a cluttered mind. And a cluttered mind equals a confused mind. Confused minds do nothing. The more organized you are, the more balanced and free you will be. We always talk about mindset and headspace—this all contributes to that.

Zoom vs. in-person meeting—what's more impactful?

Network marketing is a belly-to-belly business, but we live in a world that has changed. People are in a hustle-and-bustle society! So, when you are building global businesses, technology can be a great friend! But if technology is overused, it can sometimes slow business down. Use it to start relationships with people, but to build it, try to balance it by being there in person too.

How do you get referrals?

The answer is always *no* if you don't ask! If your prospect isn't ready to join you, you can always ask, "Who do you know (friends, coworkers, or family) who might be as excited as you are to hear about this product or opportunity?" Also, use the three magic words: "Bring a friend."

What do you pick yourself up when you're feeling down?

We can choose our thoughts, how we feel at any given moment and circumstance. So when doubt comes in, you're allowing it to come in. Happiness is a choice. We can choose to be happy or miserable despite what's going on. If you're dealing with depression, you're allowing yourself to focus on it. You can choose not to give energy to it.

How do you bounce back from a slow month?

Most important thing to acknowledge is that network marketing is like *any* other business. Think of Starbucks. Not every month will be as successful as a previous one. Some months will be better than others! So choose to have different dialogue in your mind. Acknowledge that some months will be more challenging. All that means is talking to more people and getting into a little more activity than you normally would in a regular month, and turn the following month into a great month. Remember, if goals are hit, *fantastic*! And if they're not, it doesn't matter, as long as you did *all* you could do (and you're being honest with yourself) to move yourself forward. Look back at how many presentations you've done, and stay laser beam focused on your *why*. Task: Look at your sponsoring numbers from the previous month, whatever that number was. The challenge is to bring in at least one more person (because that's growth).

What does a typical workday look like?

We have three objectives in business, and our schedule should really be centred on these three things:

- create more customers
- create more distributors
- increase the number of repeat orders

Personally, I always scheduled two to three meetings/day (one may consist of training for a team member). Lots of this work can be done from a laptop at home or meeting people for coffee. Create a schedule that works for *you*. Write down each day, "Who did I talk to?" and "What did I do?" There should be a minimum of forty-five minutes of activity each day and thirty minutes of "self-development" (but during off-peak hours, when you're unable to meet with a prospect). Also, be sure to schedule family time. We are building with our family, not in spite of them. Don't be that person who kisses them goodbye and sees them in three years.

How do you leverage your time?

If you already have a full-time job, think in terms of groups. For example, have group coffee meetings (as opposed to several individual ones). For team training, you can do ten-minute group trainings (and have other people from other teams on the call too).

What's the fastest way to the top?

Attending your main company convention for a weekend is the equivalent to working with your upline for a *year*! It's a nonnegotiable for anyone serious. Attending this (and getting your team to this) will catapult your business like nothing else. It is the number-one way to make money and build belief in you and others.

How do you increase product/service sales?

Prospects are always thinking, "What's in it for me?" So, rather than talking just facts, talk about the benefits. People buy benefits. And remember, "facts tell; stories sell." Give testimonials. And, of course, always use your product or service in public—this is a great conversation starter.

How do you motivate your team?

This was a trick question. It's not our job to motivate our team. If you have to motivate people, they aren't the right people. You are looking for self-starters with a huge desire to make a change in their life. You will know you found your superstar when they are booking their schedules with tons of income-producing activity and attending meetings, without you having to tell them.

SCRIPTS

Warm Market

Friends and Family In Your Network

Several different examples of scripts are outlined below to use in various scenarios. Please note, these are a *general* guideline; you'll want to infuse your own personality into it. The goal should always be to create *curiosity*.

Voicemail:

"Hi, Mary. Hope all is well. I wanted to chat with you about something important. Can you give me a call as soon as you have a minute? Thanks so much!"

Invite to a coffee *or* meeting via social media (Facebook, etc.):

"Hey, Mary, how are you? It's been a while. Would love to catch up. Listen, I've been meaning to talk to you about something—I'm working on something big. Not sure if it would be something you're into, but I'd love to run it by you to get your feedback. If you're open to it, let's do coffee this week?"

Reaching Out via Social Media

Samples:

"Hey, Mary. I notice we have a lot of similar interests. I love what you're about. I'd love to get together with you to tell you a bit more about what I do."

"Hey, how are you? Looks like you are doing some big things with your life! That's awesome! I also see that you're a nurse (or a realtor, etc.). How's that going for you? I actually work with a lot of nurses (or real estate agents, etc.), and I help them earn an extra income on the side. Would that be something you're open to hearing more about?"

"I love what you're about! If I gave you some information on what I do, would you be willing to take a look? Because I truly believe that you would be great at it."

"You're always at the gym, taking care of yourself (pick something about them). I love what you're about. You would be amazing at what I do! If I gave you some information, would you be willing to hear more?"

Note:

The goal when using social media is to look through your friends list and see what people are up to and who might have a possible need. You can find out a lot about people based on their pictures and what they post. If you happen to like something they post, instead of commenting, you can send them a private message. This starts to build more of a personal relationship.

Maybe you are brand new and nervous about booking a meeting?

You can say, "I've just started a new business, and I am really nervous. Before I get going, I need to practise on someone I know. Would you mind if I practised on you?"

Other Scenarios

What to say when they ask you the famous question: "What is it?"

Answer their question without going over your entire opportunity. Remember, you want to leave people *curious* so you can book a proper meeting. So to answer their question, you can say something like this:

"I show people how to make a full-time income working part-time hours. Generally, your role would be to educate people on _____ (mention your industry, e.g., health and wellness, beauty). There's also a sales component, and full training would be provided."

I would then go into "why I thought of them in *particular*." The key is to answer their question, but be *brief*, and focus on the *benefits* too.

The benefits of this industry is what really intrigues people, so mention to them (flexible schedule, lucrative income, travel, etc). If you see they are interested, you can then go on to say, "Would the daytimes work for you, or would evenings be better?" If someone is not interested, you can respond, "No worries. Just thought we could just see what's going on in each other's lives, since it's been awhile." Then back off on the opportunity and build rapport from there.

Cold Market

Follow Up

"Hi, Sarah. Just touching base on our last conversation. I'm just going over my schedule here and have a few openings this week. I'm wondering what your schedule is like. Would daytimes work for you, or would evenings be better? Looking forward to reviewing this with you to see if it might be a fit!"

Prospecting

"Do you keep your options open in terms of earning another stream of income? You'd be awesome at what I do!"

"Would you be open to hearing about something that you can do on your own schedule from home? You'd be so great at what I do."

Indirect Approach

"Would you happen to know anyone who might be looking to make an extra $1,500 on the side? I'm looking for two to three candidates."

After the Initial Meeting

What did you like best? On a scale of one to ten, where do you see yourself in terms of this being a fit for you? Hypothetically, if you were to get involved, how much would you need to earn per month to make it worth your time? How many hours per week would you be able to commit to? How many months would you be willing to work for?

"If I ... would you ..." Script (fill in the blanks with their answers)

"If I were to show you a way to make ____ (amount of money), working ____ (amount of hours) for ____ (number of months), would this be something you'd be willing to commit to?"

Success Tips

- This business is all about managing conversations. The more conversations you have, the more your business starts to move. If you're not "creating" any conversations, your business stops.
- Focus on building a bit of rapport (whether it's online or offline) so that you're not randomly messaging people out of the blue.
- People are quicker to respond by text (especially Gen Y's).
- The goal is to book an appointment within forty-eight hours of meeting someone in your cold market.
- The fortune is in the follow-up. People will join you after the fifth to twelfth exposure. Therefore, if they don't join, book next exposure (always be booking a meeting from a meeting so you're not left wondering how to reach out to someone again).
- Detach yourself from the outcome, and always remember, whoever you are looking for is out there looking for you too!

PUBLIC SPEAKING TIPS

Mindset

Choose faith over fear. If you're feeling worried and stressed, it's because you're focusing on yourself and not serving others. Take yourself out of the equation. Think about how many lives you are *not* touching if you're choosing doubt! It's not fair to others. People need you.

Get Real

Be yourself. Be honest. Say what needs to be said. Share your successes *and* failures. People will respect you for your success but *love* you for your failures!

Don't Be Too Perfect

People don't want to perceive you as an actor. They won't believe you. It's okay to say "um and uh!" because people actually talk like that!

Make a Point and Share a Story

Stories connect people. Facts tell; stories sell. So wrap everything into a story of real network marketers you know (or know of) that relates to the life situations of the various prospects you will encounter. Stories shut off the logical part of the mind and people remember them more!

Say It, Don't Read It

Make it conversational. Saying it brings what you're saying to life (college professors sound like they're reading). The messenger is more important than the message. It's all about the delivery.

Lighten Up!

Don't take yourself too seriously. Smile! People want to have fun!

Slow Down

Especially when you are saying something important. This is the most common error people make!

Conviction

Tonality and body language is 90 percent of communication! Learn how to raise and lower the tone of your voice. Make people laugh (or cry), because it's less about what you're actually saying and more about how you're making people feel. Even if you don't feel like smiling or being happy, do it anyway! Not only will it automatically get you into a better mood, but you're a leader, and leaders serve! In terms of body language, you can do anything as long as it doesn't distract the audience.

Record Yourself and Go Back and Listen

Do you convey confidence? Are you painting the picture the way you want to? Put yourself in the prospects shoes. Would you be interested? What would you change?

Repetition

Present. Review. Get better. Present. Review. Get better. You'll be amazed at the improvement you make over time. Like any skill, becoming a brilliant presenter takes a lot of time to master, but I promise you that it is so worth it and will benefit you as you carry this skill into many other areas of your life. Remember, you are the messenger! Share yourself with people, and speak belief over yourself. Collect stories, and paint a huge vision for people. Prospects will *feel* what it is like to be financially independent if you can effectively tell the story of somebody who has become financially independent from your opportunity. If you're talking about your product, include amazing results that people have gotten from them and the way their lives have improved because of your product/service.

LAST THING

Connect

Visit my blog, deborahlobart.com

Follow me on Instagram @deborahlobart

Find me on facebook:

www.facebook.com/DeborahLobartPage

ACKNOWLEDGEMENTS

This is probably the most important part of the book, where I get to express my gratitude to all those who shared a part in my journey.

First and foremost, a big thank you goes out to my husband, Adir, for constantly being there through thick and thin. If it weren't for you, my achievements wouldn't have been possible.

A huge thank you to my mom and dad for the love, ongoing support, and encouragement that I can accomplish anything I set my mind on. I love you.

A big shout-out to my beautiful children, Gabriella and Bobby, who remind me to always live life to the fullest. You are my *why* and my reason for always striving to be the best that I can be.

To all my rock star leaders, thank you for being a part of my life and blazing a trail to inspire countless people to live life by design. I appreciate you so much.

Finally, thank you to the countless mentors, leaders, and coaches who have been instrumental in my self-development journey. I have learned so much from all of you, and I am eternally grateful.

Deborah, XO

ABOUT THE AUTHOR

Deborah Lobart has been a network marketer for the last decade and has inspired hundreds of leaders to create a lifestyle of freedom through network marketing. She's achieved remarkable success and has been recognized for various top-level awards. She is also a certified life and health coach and has appeared in publications, such as Thrive Global and Fit after 45.

Deborah is a wife and mother of two. When she's not spending time with her family and friends, you can find her working out at the gym, enjoying a green smoothie, reading a good book, or traveling someplace warm.

To learn more, please visit *www.deborahlobart.com*

Insta: @deborahlobart
FB: DeborahLobartPage

www.ingramcontent.com/pod-product-compliance
Lightning Source LLC
Chambersburg PA
CBHW020434220526
45464CB00002B/702